A Sea of Grass

THE TALLGRASS PRAIRIE

by David Dvorak, Jr.

MACMILLAN PUBLISHING COMPANY · NEW YORK
MAXWELL MACMILLAN CANADA · TORONTO
MAXWELL MACMILLAN INTERNATIONAL
NEW YORK · OXFORD · SINGAPORE · SYDNEY

To my nieces Lindsay, Maria, and Emily, my nephews Richard and Michael,
and to all the other children of the world, who deserve to have the various ecosystems
of the planet left in a natural condition that they can enjoy and understand.

I would like to thank the staff of the Brecksville Nature Center of Cleveland Metroparks for giving me their time and assistance in creating this book. Senior naturalist Karl Smith, along with naturalists Sophie Cayless and Mary Haffner, offered many useful suggestions. Everyone associated with the Konza Prairie Research Natural Area, operated by Kansas State University, was very helpful. Special thanks also to the many students of the East Cleveland schools who have shared in the learning process with me.

—D. D.

Macmillan Publishing Company is part of the Maxwell Communication Group of Companies.
Macmillan Publishing Company, 866 Third Avenue, New York, NY 10022
Maxwell Macmillan Canada, Inc., 1200 Eglinton Avenue East, Suite 200, Don Mills, Ontario M3C 3N1
First edition. Printed in the United States of America

10 9 8 7 6 5 4 3 2 1

The text of this book is set in 14 point Palatino. Book design by Constance Ftera.

Library of Congress Cataloging-in-Publication Data
Dvorak, David.   A sea of grass : the tallgrass prairie / David Dvorak, Jr. — 1st ed.   p.   cm.
Summary: Describes the plants and animals that live on the prairie and what takes place there during the different seasons.
ISBN 0-02-733245-4
1. Prairies—Great Plains—Juvenile literature.   2. Prairie ecology—Great Plains—Juvenile literature.
[1. Prairies.   2. Prairie ecology.   3. Seasons.]   I. Title.
QH104.5.G73D96   1994   508.315′3′0978—dc20   93-19507

Grass, tallgrass, moving with the wind.
Prairie grasses reaching for the sky.

The prairie stretches to the horizon, a sea of tallgrass.

A herd of buffalo moves across the prairie, feeding on grasses.

A badger sniffs the air in search of animals it feeds on, such as ground squirrels, mice, gophers, and voles. The badger can dig animals out of their underground dens with its sharp claws.

The prairie changes with the seasons. Plants turn shades of green as they produce food for themselves during the summer growing season.

In autumn, as the days become shorter and the temperature cools, the food made by the prairie plants passes down the stems and is stored in the roots. The plants then turn a golden brown.

Some plants, like sneezeweed and fringed gentian, flower in the autumn, adding color to the prairie.

In late autumn heavy frosts cover the plants. Only the seed head of the wild bergamot flower now remains. Seeds fall to the ground and often become food for birds, insects, and rodents. Plants produce many seeds, and those that live will become new plants next spring.

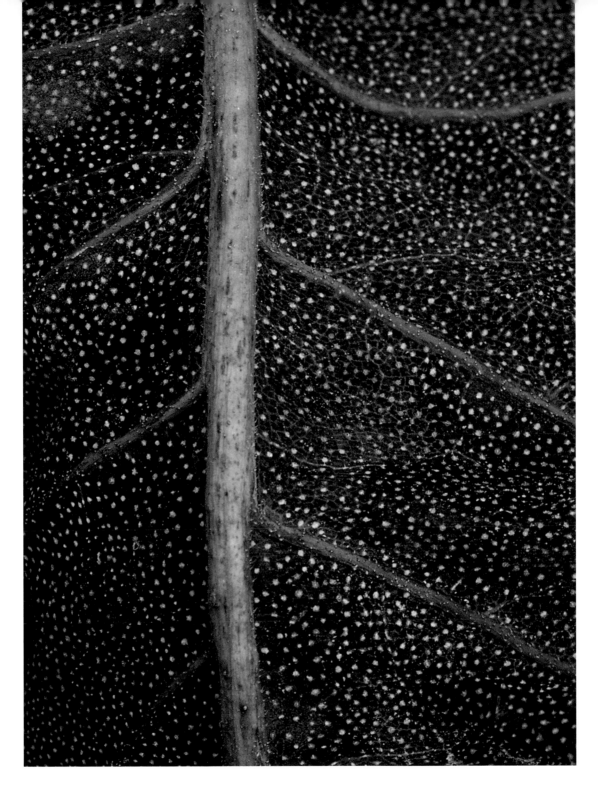

As autumn progresses, leaves of the prairie dock plant turn brown when the food-making process in the leaves comes to an end.

Many animals, like the thirteen-lined ground squirrel, feed heavily in autumn, putting on extra weight for the coming of winter. The ground squirrel hibernates, living off the fat stored in its body.

Another animal that is inactive during the winter is the horned lizard, which lives in rocky areas of the prairie. Like the ground squirrel, it will spend the cold months underground.

The winds of winter arrive from the north, bringing snow that piles into drifts. Winter is a season of rest for the prairie plants.

The tops of plants sticking up through the snow have died, but their roots remain alive in the soil under the snow cover. The roots grow several feet into the earth and, holding the soil together, make the thick prairie sod.

Spring arrives with warm south winds. Thunderstorms form and bring heavy rains.

In early spring and late fall, lightning may start fires. Their deep roots keep prairie plants from being harmed. Many prairie plants even grow and flower more after a fire.

The prairie is soon a green sea stretching to the horizon.

The pasqueflower and prairie shooting star bloom in spring, adding bright color to the prairie.

Grasses begin growing rapidly and are dark green by late spring.

A young buffalo feeds on the rich milk provided by its mother.

A young cottontail rabbit leaves its shelter to explore on its own.

A black-tailed jackrabbit looks over the prairie. While rabbits feed on plants, they must keep watch for their predators—badgers and hawks—which would like to make a meal of them.

Summer is the season of greatest growth and activity on the prairie. During the summer most plants flower, dotting the deep green cover of the prairie with colorful blossoms. As the tallgrass prairie plants are growing to heights of five to eight feet, animals are busy raising their young.

Big bluestem

Switchgrass

Grasses cover most of the prairie. In summer most grasses flower, and depend on the wind to move their pollen from one plant to another. When the pollen reaches the right spot, it will produce seeds so more grass can grow next year.

Prairie cordgrass

Indian grass

Purple coneflower

Butterfly milkweed

Wildflowers in many shapes and sizes live among the grasses. Animals from grasshoppers to deer feed on the wildflowers as well as on the grasses. Most wildflowers are pollinated by insects, not the wind.

Compass plant

Sensitive briar

Insects and spiders make their homes and find food in the prairie. Bees and butterflies visit flowers in search of nectar, a sweet-smelling liquid made by many flowers. Their search turns them into plant pollinators.

Honeybee

Monarch

Grasshoppers graze on the leaves of plants, while spiders wait on their webs. Eventually an unlucky insect is trapped in the web and becomes food for the spider.

Many birds that live on the prairie feed on plant seeds or on the many types of insects. The upland sandpiper and eastern kingbird use their long bills to capture insects.

Bobwhite quail and dickcissels use their thicker bills to crush the plant seeds they depend on for food.

Other animals live on the prairie, too. A white-tailed deer buck looks over the grasslands, as a doe and fawns browse on prairie plants.

Buffalo are the largest grazing animals living on the prairie. These symbols of the North American grasslands once roamed in huge herds in their search for food. Overhunting and loss of habitat to farms and ranches brought them near extinction. Rescued by conservationists, they now live in some national parks, wildlife refuges, and prairie preserves.

Year in, year out, the prairie grass rolls like a sea, waves of grass in the wind.

Just a little over 150 years ago tallgrass prairie covered approximately 240 million acres of midwestern North America. From prairie patches in Ohio to the vast unbroken prairie that began in western Indiana, tallgrass prairie dominated the landscape over the eastern third of the North American grasslands. Although estimates vary, it is likely that less than one percent of this area remains as tallgrass prairie now, making it an endangered ecosystem. The rich, dark soils created by the decay of tallgrass prairie plants were converted by plows into the agricultural area known today as the corn belt. It is ironic that many of the first Europeans to pass through the prairies thought them to be infertile because they lacked trees.

Today many prairie remnants are only tiny patches of land left along railroad lines or around pioneer cemeteries. But restoration of land to tallgrass prairie has been making increasing headway in the past twenty years. From the first prairie restoration, inspired by Aldo Leopold at the University of Wisconsin–Madison in the 1930s, to current restorations, more and more land is being converted from weed patch or cornfield to tallgrass prairie. The Nature Conservancy, a private organization dedicated to saving natural areas, has made the tallgrass prairie a priority. There are now prairie preserves in many states and provinces, largely as a result of work done by this organization and state departments of natural resources.

Most of the photos in this book were taken at the Konza Prairie Research Natural Area near Manhattan, Kansas, which was purchased by the Nature Conservancy. A good way to gain information about visiting tallgrass prairie areas is to write to or call the prairie preserves and restorations listed below, which have areas open to the public. The Bigelow and Smith State Nature Preserves in Ohio and the Rochester Preserve in Iowa are excellent examples of prairie left around gravestones. Tallgrass prairie restorations can be viewed at the University of Wisconsin–Madison Arboretum, the Shaw Arboretum, and the Brecksville Nature Center.

Bigelow and Smith Cemeteries/State Nature Preserves
Ohio Department of Natural Resources
Division of Natural Areas and Preserves
1889 Fountain Square, Columbus, OH 43224
(614) 265-6453

Brecksville Nature Center
Part of the Cleveland Metroparks
9305 Brecksville Road, Brecksville, OH 44141
(216) 526-1012

Chiwaukee Prairie
The Nature Conservancy, Wisconsin Chapter
333 West Mifflin Street, Suite 107, Madison, WI 53703
(608) 251-8140

Konza Prairie Research Natural Area
Konza Prairie
Manhattan, KS 66502
(913) 532-6615 or 532-6820

The Nature Conservancy
Tallgrass Prairie Preserve
P.O. Box 458, Pawhuska, OK 74056
(918) 287-4803

Niawathe Prairie
The Nature Conservancy, Missouri Chapter
2800 South Brentwood Boulevard
St. Louis, MO 61344
(314) 968-1105

Rochester Cemetery, Rochester, IA
(Take Exit 267 off Interstate 80; follow
Route 38 North about ¾ mile north of I-80.)

Shaw Arboretum
P.O. Box 38, Gray Summit, MO 63069
(314) 742-3512

University of Wisconsin–Madison Arboretum
1207 Seminole Highway, Madison, WI 53711
(608) 263-7888